and sometimes I live with my dad,
in our flat, right at the top!

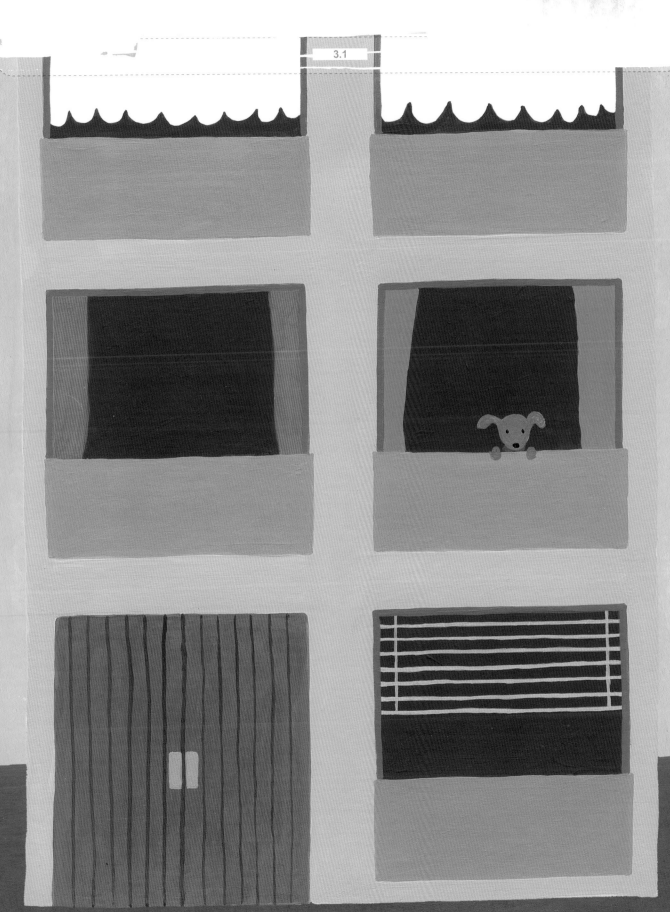

I chose yellow walls for my bedroom at my mum's house ...

and flowery wallpaper
for my bedroom at my dad's.

My mum and dad both
know I don't like going
to sleep in the dark.
So at my mum's I have a
panda night light ...

I keep some toys at my mum's house
and some at my dad's ...

My mum always used to collect me from school ...

Sometimes my dad takes me

camping at the weekend ...

when I was in
my school play...

my mum and dad
both came to watch me.

On my birthday
my mum made
me a cake ...

If I am missing my mum or my dad ...

My mum and dad
love me a lot and
so do all my family.

UNCLE BRIAN

LiTTLe FLORA

COUSIN RUBY

This book belongs to

....

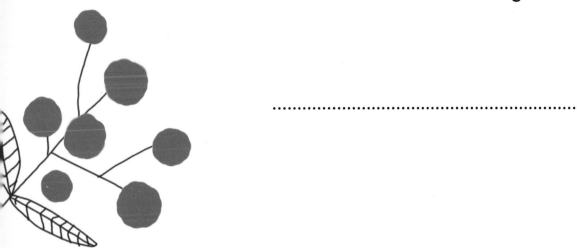

Written by Rosie Greening.
Illustrated by Lara Ede.

Mermaid Mia

and the Royal Visit

Lara Ede · Rosie Greening

make
believe
ideas

Mermaid Mia loved to write

new **stories** every day.

She ran the **paper** at her school with **Emily** and **Fay**.

Emily took the **photographs** . . .

Say cheese!

and Fay did the **reviews**.

The Mermail

But **Mia** was the one in charge of each day's **front-page** news.

One morning, **Mia** longed to find a juicy piece of **news.**

She got her **pad** and went in **search** of **something** she could use.

Her first lead was a story
on the **snails** in the canteen.

Gross!

But the **news** was **so** s-l-o-w – m-o-v-i-n-g, Mia **really** wasn't keen.

Then she heard a **rumour** of a **whale** stuck in the **gym**.

"Now **that's** a story," **Mia** thought. "I'll write my news on him!"

But just as **Mia** reached the **whale**, he managed to get **out**.

"My front page will be bare!" she cried.
"What can I write about?"

Suddenly, a sneaky thought **popped** into **Mia's** head.

"The **real** news isn't good enough –
I'll **make it up** instead!"

She **swam** back to the newsroom
and began to type at speed.

"This **news** will make a **splash**," she thought.
"They're **sure** to want a read!"

Queen Marina is one of the most popular royals under the sea. Whether it's recycling in the coral beds or opening libraries, the queen always has a new project on the go. Just last month, it was Queen Marina's birthday. It was a magical day, with tasty treats, a fantastic band and comedy from the clownfish.

The biggest gift Queen Marina received was a beautiful carriage, though it has yet to be used out in public. We believe she is saving it for a special occasion...

The Mermail

As soon as it was printed, **Mia's** words began to **spread**,

STARFISH ACADEMY

and the school **buzzed** with **excitement** at the **front-page** news that said . . .

The Mermail

Queen Marina

The Royal Palace

A ROYAL VISIT!

Written by Mermaid Mia

Her Highness, Queen Marina will be visiting our school. She's heard of the academy and wants to meet us all!

It was all the **mermaids** talked about: the **best** news of the year!

In class, they'd whisper **happily**: "The **Queen** is coming HERE!"

I can't wait!

I bet we'll have a ball.

But soon the **news** got out of hand, which made poor **Mia** fret.
And as the day drew closer, she kept **hoping** they'd **forget**.

With one week left, she told her friends:

"I've made a **big mistake.**
The **queen's** not **really** visiting –
the news I wrote was **fake!**"

"You **should** have told the **truth**," said Fay.
"But now we need a **plan**.
We'll tell the queen what happened
and then **fix** this if we can."

So **Mia** sent a **letter**
to the queen's **royal** address.

Queen Marina
The Royal Palace
Under the Sea

Collections:
Mon–Fri
7am

Please do not
put shells in
the postbox.

She asked the queen to **help** them out,
and **hoped** that she'd say **yes**.

Soon, the **royal whale mail** delivered them a note.

You've got mail!

Mermaid Mia
Starfish Academy
Under the Sea

It was signed "Love, **Queen Marina**,"
and this is what she wrote . . .

Dear Mia,

You're very brave for owning up —
it's not easy to do.
And thank you for inviting me,
I'd love to visit you!

Love,
Queen Marina

At last, the **special** day arrived:
the **mermaids** couldn't wait.

YOU'RE GREAT!

They lined the school with **pretty flags,**
and a **sign** that said, "YOU'RE GREAT!"

A **carriage** pulled by **dolphins** soon drew up and parked outside.

She waved to me!

I love her crown.

The **queen** swam up to meet them all, and Mia **beamed** with **pride**.

The day was so **amazing**, Mia knew what she **should** do.

Miss Isabella meets Queen Marina

The Queen's new fitness plan is a slam dunk!

Star student shows off her winning formula

The Queen receives a warm welcome

She put the story in the **news**, and every word was **true**.

Everyone had a sea-riously good time!

Snail surprise

A ROYAL SUCCESS!

Written by Mermaid Mia

We had a great time yesterday
with Queen Marina here.
And as she left, she told us all:
"I'll come again next year!"

After that, **Mia** was **truthful**,
even when the news was **slow**.

The Mermail

SHELL SHOCK:
Snails spotted
in the canteen!

She'd **learnt** that being **honest**
was the **only** way to **go!**